The Library of the PILGRIMS

A Plymouth Partnership:
Pilgrims and Native Americans

Susan Whitehurst

The Rosen Publishing Group's
PowerKids Press™
New York

Dedicated to Meggie, an EMT Angel

Published in 2002 by The Rosen Publishing Group, Inc.
29 East 21st Street, New York, NY 10010

First Edition

Book Design: Maria E. Melendez
Project Editor: Frances E. Ruffin

Photo Credits: Title page (Native American in full war costume), pp. 4, 5, 7, 8, 17, 20 © North Wind Pictures;
title page (Samoset on his first visit to Plymouth Colony), pp. 12, 15, 16, 19 © The Granger Collection;
title page (Massasoit and the Puritans), pp. 9, 11 © CORBIS/Bettmann.

Whitehurst, Susan.
A Plymouth partnership : Pilgrims and native Americans / Susan Whitehurst.
    p. cm. — (The library of the Pilgrims)
Includes bibliographical references and index.
ISBN 0-8239-5810-8 (lib. bdg.)
  1. Pilgrims (New Plymouth Colony)—History—Juvenile literature. 2. Indians of North America—Massachusetts—History—Colonial period, ca.
1600–1775—Juvenile literature. 3. Massachusetts—History—New Plymouth, 1620–1691—Juvenile literature.
  [1. Pilgrims (New Plymouth Colony) 2. Indians of North America—Massachusetts—History—Colonialperiod, ca. 1600–1775.
  3. Massachusetts—History—New Plymouth, 1620–1691.] I. Title.
F68 .W593 2002
974.4'8202—dc21

2001000251

Manufactured in the United States of America

Contents

1 A New Land and New People   5

2 A Close Watch   6

3 "Welcome, Englishmen"   9

4 A Partnership Begins   10

5 A Peace Treaty   13

6 Squanto, a Special Friend   14

7 Lessons with Squanto   17

8 A Lost Boy and a Bellyache   18

9 A Feast of Friendship   21

10 A Treaty Ends, a Nation Begins   22

Glossary   23

Index   24

Web Sites   24

A New Land and New People

When the *Mayflower* sailed into Cape Cod, Massachusetts, on November 19, 1620, the 102 Pilgrims on board the ship saw a rocky, cold, and not-very-friendly-looking land. The **voyage** had taken 66 days. Many of the people on the *Mayflower* were happy to see any land at all. Several Pilgrim men explored the coast to find a place to live. When they came ashore, they saw a few Native American men who hurried away into the woods. The Pilgrims, who had never met Native Americans, were afraid of them.

Some Native Americans, like the man above, watched the *Mayflower* ship sail into Cape Cod.

◀ As they sailed into Cape Cod, the Pilgrims aboard the *Mayflower* were happy to see land.

A Close Watch

When the Pilgrims went ashore, they heard sounds, but didn't see anyone. Suddenly Native American arrows flew at them, and they returned fire with their **muskets**, but no one was hurt.

The Pilgrims would not see the Indians again for several months, until March 1621. The Native Americans were curious about the Pilgrims, though. They kept a very close watch on what was going on in Plymouth **Colony**. The Pilgrims' new neighbors were the Wampanoag, a Native American people who had lived in southeastern Massachusetts for thousands of years.

The Wampanoag people knew that white men could mean trouble. In the past, they had kidnapped Native Americans and had brought disease, such as smallpox, that wiped out entire villages.

The Pilgrims brought their families with them and were building homes. They planned to stay. ▶

"Welcome, Englishmen"

The Pilgrims suffered a long, hard, cold winter. Half of them died from illness. When spring came, they were just beginning to feel better. That's when a Native American man named Samoset walked into their town. The Pilgrims were shocked. He said, "Welcome, Englishmen. I'm Samoset." He spoke English! He carried two arrows, one with an arrowhead and one without. This meant, "I come in peace or in war, it's your choice." Samoset had learned English from Englishmen who had sailed there to fish. Massasoit, the Wampanoag chief, had sent Samoset to say hello and to find out who the Pilgrims were.

◀ Samoset, a Native American, met the Pilgrims who had come from England.

This is a statue of Massasoit in Plymouth, Massachusetts.

A Partnership Begins

Samoset explained that Plymouth used to be a Wampanoag village called Pawtuxet. All of the people in the village had died of a **plague**. He said Chief Massasoit wanted to meet and trade animal furs with them. This was good news. The Pilgrims had promised to send back furs to England to repay the **merchants** who had lent them money to make the trip on the *Mayflower*. On March 22, 1621, Samoset returned to Plymouth with Chief Massasoit and 60 Wampanoag men! At first the Pilgrims were worried. They had settled on Native American land. Did the Native Americans want the Pilgrims to move?

Chief Massasoit and 60 of his men welcomed the Pilgrims.

In 1621, there were 24,000 Wampanoag in the Plymouth area and only 50 Pilgrims.

A Peace Treaty

When Chief Massasoit came to visit, the Pilgrims put together a welcoming gift. They gave him two knives, a copper chain with a jewel, and some butter. Edward Winslow gave the gifts to Chief Massasoit and invited him to meet their governor, John Carver.

Governor Carver and Massasoit met in a half-finished Pilgrim house. They ate, drank, and talked all afternoon. They made a peace treaty. In the treaty, they agreed never to hurt each other, never to bring weapons when they visited, and to help each other if someone else attacked them. Then they smoked a peace pipe and drank **brandy**.

Governor John Carver and Chief Massasoit agreed to keep peace between the Pilgrims and the Wampanoag.

The peace treaty made between Pilgrim Governor John Carver and Wampanoag Chief Massasoit lasted for more than 50 years.

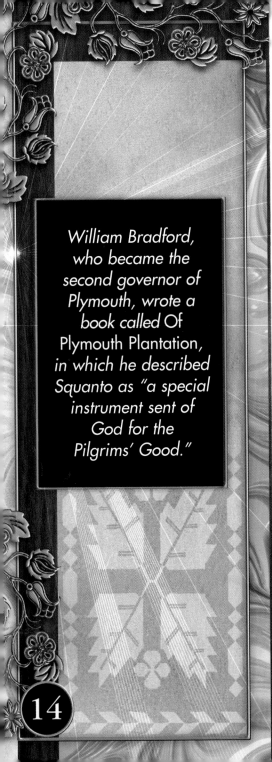

William Bradford, who became the second governor of Plymouth, wrote a book called Of Plymouth Plantation, in which he described Squanto as "a special instrument sent of God for the Pilgrims' Good."

Squanto, a Special Friend

Carver and Massasoit couldn't have made the peace treaty or even talked together without the help of one very special Native American man, named Squanto. Squanto was a member of the Pawtuxet people. He had been kidnapped in 1614, by Captain Thomas Hunt and had been taken to Spain as a **slave**. After several years, he was taken to England where he learned English. When Squanto finally sailed home, he found that all of his people were dead. He became an **interpreter** for the Pilgrims and the Wampanoag. Squanto lived with the Pilgrims until his death in 1622.

This image of Squanto is from an American lithograph created in 1873. ▶

Lessons with Squanto

Growing and catching food was the Pilgrims' biggest problem. Squanto taught them to plant corn. He showed them how to plant a few corn seeds in a little hill of dirt with a few dead fish to help the corn grow. The Pilgrims also were having a hard time catching fish with the big hooks that they had brought from England. Squanto showed them how to fish with a net. He also taught them to feel along a river bottom with their feet to find an eel in the mud, and how to spear it. He pointed out which plants and berries were good for eating, how to tap maple trees for syrup, and how to trap animals for meat.

◀ *Squanto showed the Pilgrims how to grow corn and other vegetables by planting seeds with dead fish.*

This brightly colored corn is called Indian corn. Squanto taught the Pilgrims to plant corn "when the oak leaves are as big as a mouse's ear."

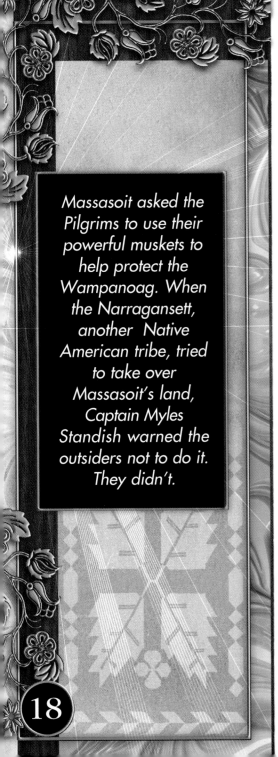

A Lost Boy and a Bellyache

The Pilgrims and the Wampanoag visited each other when they were sick or in trouble. When a 16-year-old Pilgrim boy, John Billington, got lost in the woods and lived on berries for five days, the Wampanoag found him. They took him safely to their village.

A Pilgrim doctor, Edward Winslow, was called to Massasoit's bedside when the chief thought he was dying. Although it was only a very bad bellyache, Winslow stayed for two days and treated him with a soup made from duck and **herbs**. Massasoit said, "I will never forget this kindness."

Chief Massasoit became a friend of Dr. Edward Winslow, who had treated Massasoit for a bad bellyache. ▶

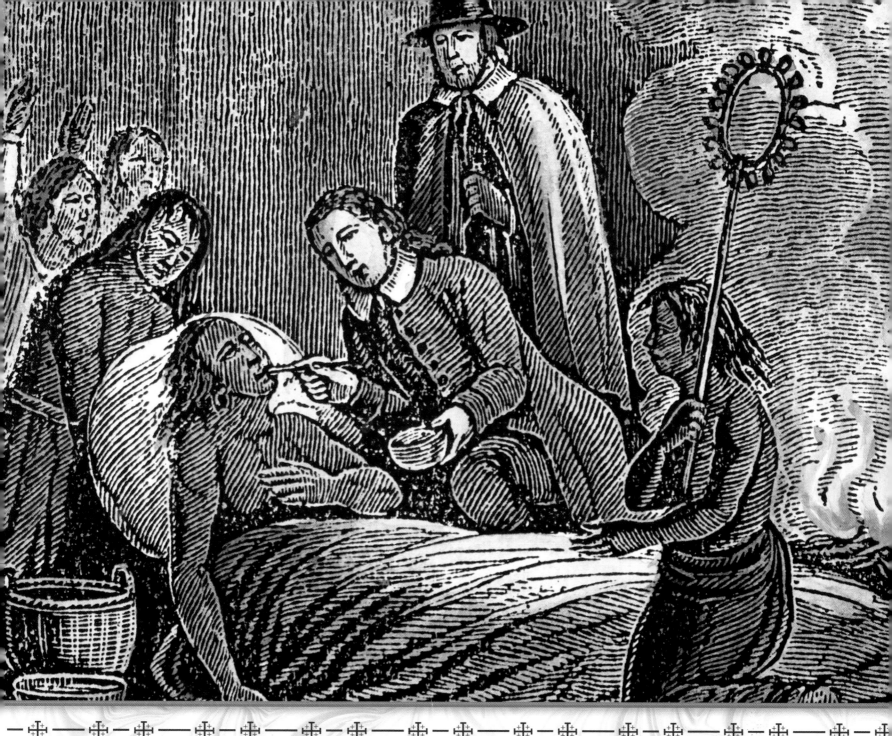

A Feast of Friendship

By working with the Wampanoag, the Pilgrims had a wonderful harvest in the fall of 1621. There was enough food to share. William Bradford, the second governor of Plymouth, said the Pilgrims should have a big harvest feast and should invite Massasoit. They were surprised when the great chief came with 90 men. To make sure that there was enough food, Massasoit sent his men into the woods to bring back five deer.

The Pilgrims and the Wampanoag were having such a good time that the feast went on for three days. They ate and played games. They danced, sang, and ran races.

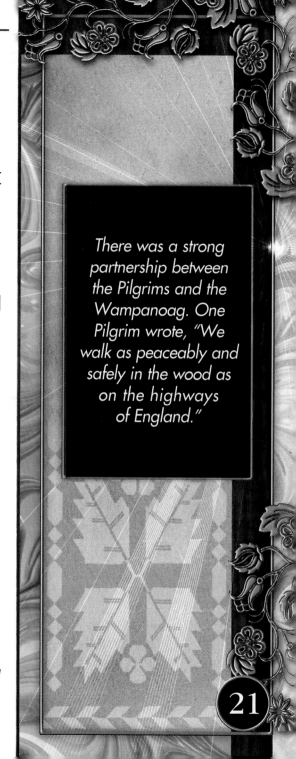

There was a strong partnership between the Pilgrims and the Wampanoag. One Pilgrim wrote, "We walk as peaceably and safely in the wood as on the highways of England."

◀ *Captain Myles Standish invited Massasoit and the Wampanoag to join the Pilgrims in a thanksgiving parade.*

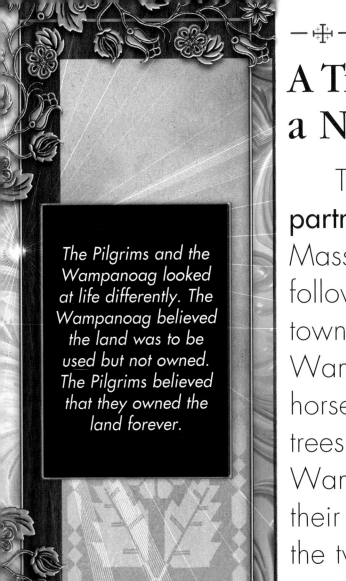

The Pilgrims and the Wampanoag looked at life differently. The Wampanoag believed the land was to be used but not owned. The Pilgrims believed that they owned the land forever.

A Treaty Ends, a Nation Begins

The Wampanoag and Pilgrim **partnership** lasted for as long as Chief Massasoit lived. More and more settlers followed the Pilgrims. They built more towns closer and closer to the Wampanoag villages. Pilgrim cows and horses ate the grass. They cut down the trees to make homes and fields. The Wampanoag were being crowded out of their own land. The differences between the two peoples meant the end of a very special friendship. It had been a friendship that had saved the lives of the Pilgrims and that had helped to begin a new nation.

Glossary

brandy (BRAN-dee) An alcoholic beverage made from wine.

colony (KAH-luh-nee) An area in a new country where a group of people move, who are still ruled by the leaders and laws of their old country.

herbs (URBZ) Plants used as medicines or for seasoning food.

interpreter (in-TER-preh-ter) A person who translates a foreign language.

merchants (MUR-chints) People who sell things.

muskets (MUS-kits) Guns with a long barrel that are used for hunting.

partnership (PART-ner-ship) Cooperation between two or more people.

plague (PLAYG) A dangerous disease that spreads quickly.

slave (SLAYV) A person who is "owned" by another person and is forced to work for him or her without pay.

voyage (VOY-ij) A journey, often by water.

Index

B

Billington, John, 18
Bradford, William, 21

C

Cape Cod,
    Massachusetts, 5
Carver, John, 13, 14
corn, 17

F

feast, 21
fish, 17
food, 17

H

Hunt, Thomas, 14

M

Massasoit, 9, 10, 13, 14,
    18, 21, 22
Mayflower, 5, 10

P

Pawtuxet, 10, 14

S

Samoset, 9, 10
settlers, 22
Squanto, 14, 17

W

Wampanoag, 6, 9, 10,
    14, 18, 21, 22
Winslow, Edward, 13, 18

Web Sites

To find out more about the Pilgrims and Native Americans, check out these Web sites:
www.pilgrimhall.org/museum.htm
www.tolatsga.org/wampa.html